Copyright © 2016 Diane M. Benner

All Rights Reserved

ISBN-13: 978-1535165167

ISBN-10: 1535165162

No part of this book may be reproduced or transmitted in any form or by any means whatsoever without express written permission from the author.

Special Appreciation to ...

Vacations at **Bay Blessed**, the most relaxing beach home on the Delaware Bay, and my inspiration for writing this book. Thank you, Tina and Joel.

It is my hope that everyone will gain respect and love for these gentle and beautiful horseshoe crabs after reading this book. Enjoy!

Diane

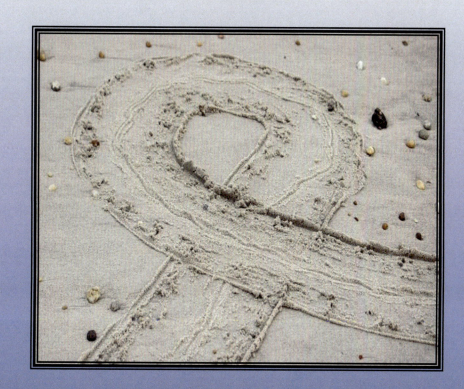

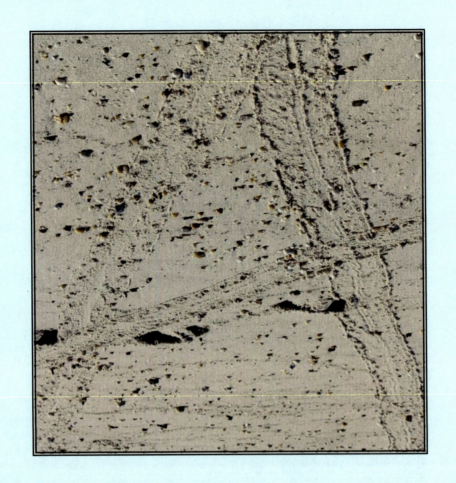

A is for alive. Horseshoe crabs have been alive on earth for a long time. They are related to the trilobites, which were alive before the time of the dinosaurs.

B is for bay. You will find the largest population of horseshoe crabs in the Delaware Bay. Female horseshoe crabs lay their eggs there each spring.

C is for crab. Horseshoe crabs are not crustaceans or even real crabs. They are related to spiders, ticks, and scorpions.

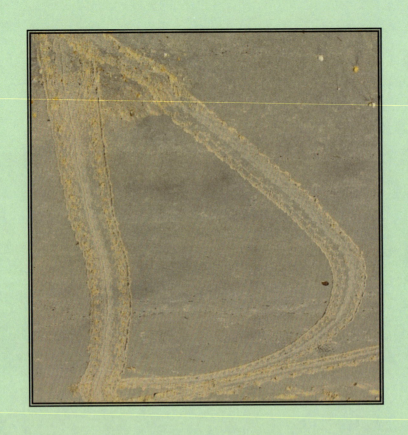

D is for drags. After she lays the eggs, the female horseshoe crab drags the male over the eggs so he can fertilize them. He uses his front claws to attach himself to the back of her shell.

E is for eggs. The female horseshoe crab can lay 60,000 or more tiny eggs in the wet sand near the water's edge. Each soft egg is about the size of a mustard seed. The young horseshoe crabs will emerge from their eggs several weeks later.

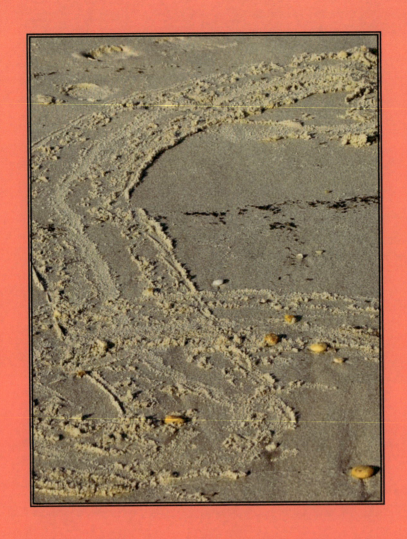

F is for five. A horseshoe crab has five pairs of legs and also has five gill flaps.

G is for gills. Horseshoe crabs have "book gills" which are used for breathing. These are thin plates that look like the pages of a book. They are found on the underside of their bodies below their legs.

H is for humans. Many human lives are saved every year because of horseshoe crabs! Their bright blue blood is used for eye research, absorbable stitches, purity tests for medicines, and helping to speed up blood clotting.

I is for important. Horseshoe crabs are important to our ocean communities. Many seabirds rely on horseshoe crab eggs for food, especially the migrating Red Knot birds.

J is for jawless. Horseshoe crabs do not have jaws to chew food. Their legs have bristles which grind up food and push it into their mouths. They also have gizzards which contain sand and some gravel to help break up their food.

K is for King Crab, just one of the many nicknames for a horseshoe crab. It is also known as a Helmet Crab, a Horsefoot Crab, and a Saucepan Crab.

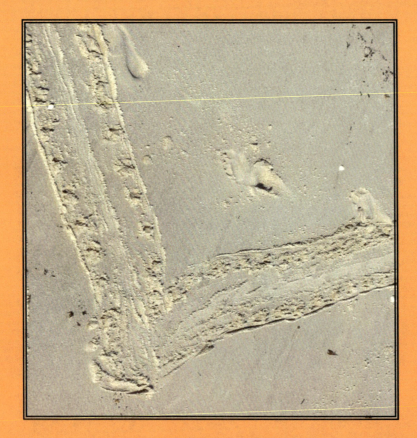

L is for larger. The female horseshoe crabs are usually larger than the males. Adult females have legs that all look the same. Males have a set of front legs that look like little boxing gloves, and are different from their other eight legs.

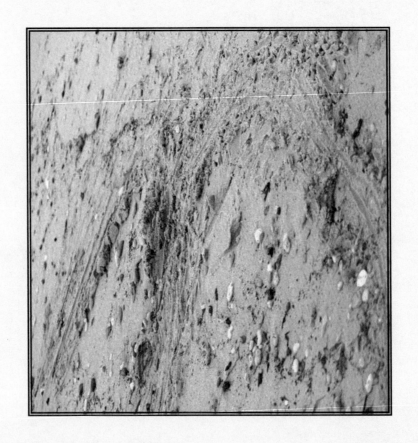

M is for molt. Horseshoe crabs shed their exoskeletons by crawling out through the front of their shells. They can molt about sixteen times before reaching adulthood. You can see these empty shells on the beach.

N is for nocturnal. Horseshoe crabs are nocturnal, which means they are more active at night. That is when they hunt for food. During the daytime, they go back to the ocean floor.

O is for oceans. There are four species of horseshoe crabs living in the oceans throughout the world. One of those species is the North American Horseshoe Crab. You will find this horseshoe crab around the eastern coast of the United States.

P is for predators. Horseshoe crabs have few natural predators. They are primarily hunted for food by sea turtles, sharks, and migratory birds. Pollution in the oceans has greatly decreased the horseshoe crab population.

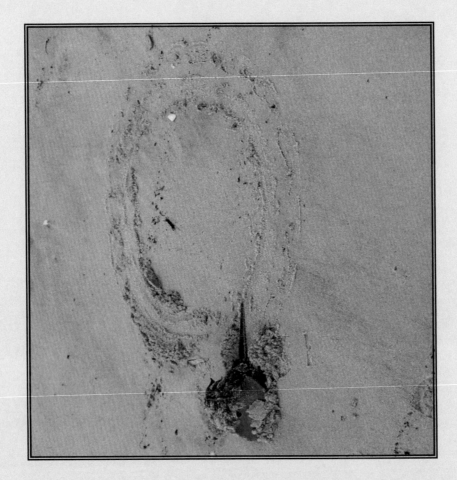

Q is for quiet. Horseshoe crabs are very quiet creatures. They do not make any type of noise to "talk" to each other. They even move quietly over the sand.

R is for report. If you find a horseshoe crab with a white tag on its shell, please report it to the organization listed on the tag. This helps researchers to track their population and migration patterns as they travel up and down the coast.

S is for save. We can all do our part to help save horseshoe crabs. Carefully pick them up by their shells and flip them over. Then watch them as they make an interesting path on their way back into the ocean.

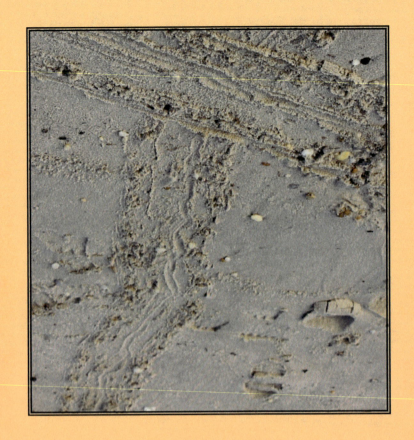

T is for telson, the tail part of a horseshoe crab. It helps to steer or change the horseshoe crab's direction when it is swimming in the ocean. If upside down on the beach, it will use its telson to try to turn itself over.

U is for upside-down. A young horseshoe crab can sometimes be found swimming upside down in the ocean.

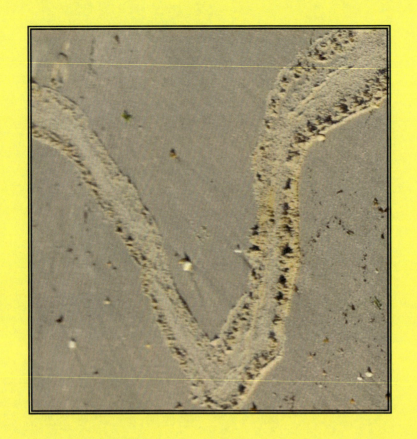

V is for vision. A horseshoe crab has many eyes. With two compound eyes and five simple eyes on the top of their shell, it can see three feet ahead. There are also two eyes near its mouth, and light sensors on its telson.

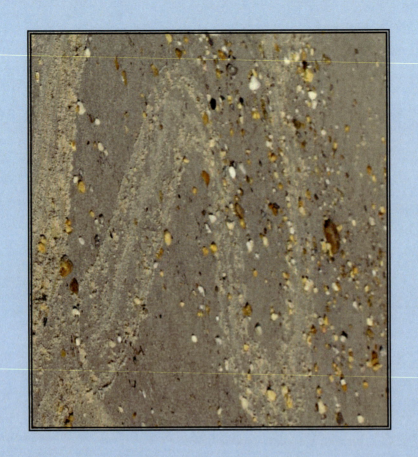

W is for without. Some horseshoe crabs can go without eating for a long time, close to twelve months. Horseshoe crabs eat mostly sea worms, clams, crabs, and small crustaceans.

X is for Xiphosura, which is the classification for horseshoe crabs. It is the Greek word for "sword tail", because their telson looks like a sword.

Y is for years. Horseshoe crabs can live to be close to twenty years old. A horseshoe crab reaches adulthood when it is about ten years old.

Z is for amaZing! Horseshoe crabs are amazing creatures because they can regrow a body part in a similar way that a starfish regrows an arm.

For more information on horseshoe crabs and how to help them, visit these sites:

http://a-z-animals.com/animals/horseshoe-crab

http://horseshoecrab.org

http://www.dnrec.delaware.gov

http://news.nationalgeographic.com

https://www.nwf.org

http://bioweb.uwlax.edu

http://en.wikipedia.org

About the Author

Diane Benner has been an elementary teacher in Pennsylvania for over 24 years. She has written several educational grants, and has been published in *Mailbox Magazine.* Fox 43 TV honored her as a SUBWAY Teacher of The Week for her community service work with her students.

An amateur photographer, she has photographed and rescued thousands of horseshoe crabs in the Delaware Bay.

Diane resides in Dover, PA, and has two adult children, Justin and Haley.

Made in the USA
Middletown, DE
01 April 2017